MAYER SMITH

Frost and Fire in Your Eyes

Copyright © 2025 by Mayer Smith

All rights reserved. No part of this publication may be reproduced, stored or transmitted in any form or by any means, electronic, mechanical, photocopying, recording, scanning, or otherwise without written permission from the publisher. It is illegal to copy this book, post it to a website, or distribute it by any other means without permission.

This novel is entirely a work of fiction. The names, characters and incidents portrayed in it are the work of the author's imagination. Any resemblance to actual persons, living or dead, events or localities is entirely coincidental.

Mayer Smith asserts the moral right to be identified as the author of this work.

Mayer Smith has no responsibility for the persistence or accuracy of URLs for external or third-party Internet Websites referred to in this publication and does not guarantee that any content on such Websites is, or will remain, accurate or appropriate.

Designations used by companies to distinguish their products are often claimed as trademarks. All brand names and product names used in this book and on its cover are trade names, service marks, trademarks and registered trademarks of their respective owners. The publishers and the book are not associated with any product or vendor mentioned in this book. None of the companies referenced within the book have endorsed the book.

First edition

This book was professionally typeset on Reedsy. Find out more at reedsy.com

Contents

1	The First Encounter	1
2	A Cold War	8
3	The Spark Ignites	14
4	Secrets Unveiled	20
5	Crossed Wires	27
6	Firestorm	33
7	Torn Between Desire and Duty	40
8	In the Eye of the Storm	47
9	A Heart's Reckoning	53
10	The Battle Within	59
11	A Love Rekindled	65
12	A New Dawn	71

One

The First Encounter

The night air was thick with the smell of impending rain, and the streets of Ashford Heights seemed to hum with a quiet tension, as though the city itself was holding its breath. Lena stood at the corner of Oliver's Bar, one of those dark, weathered establishments that had survived decades of change. The neon sign buzzed erratically above her, casting a sickly green glow over the scene. People moved in and out, their silhouettes obscured by the smoke that curled from the door like ghosts.

Lena was used to this part of the city—the gritty, broken side that people avoided. But tonight, something felt different. The sense of danger that had always simmered in the background was now at the forefront, and her nerves buzzed with a quiet, restless energy. She pulled the collar of her leather jacket tighter around her neck, a futile attempt to ward off the chill that had crept beneath her skin.

She had come here for answers. To find the one person who could unlock the door to the mysteries that had followed her family for generations. Her breath hitched at the thought. She hadn't been searching for anything so dangerous before, but tonight, her father's last words echoed in her mind, as clear as if he were standing beside her.

"Find him, Lena. He's the key."

Lena wasn't sure if the "him" in question was a man or a myth, but she wasn't about to let the possibility slip through her fingers. She had grown up in this city, breathing its secrets, hearing its whispers. And tonight, she would find out just how deep those secrets went.

The door swung open, and the sound of laughter and clinking glasses spilled into the street. Lena's eyes narrowed as she stepped inside, immediately enveloped by the thick haze of cigarette smoke and the sound of a blues guitar playing low in the background. The bar was dimly lit, with shadows dancing across the worn wood floors. A pool table sat in the corner, and a handful of patrons lingered over drinks, their voices a low murmur that blended into the atmosphere.

But it wasn't the people that drew Lena's attention—it was him.

He was standing at the far end of the bar, leaning against the counter as if the weight of the world rested on his shoulders. The man's presence was magnetic, his every movement deliberate, as though he knew how much attention he commanded. His face was hidden in the shadow of a wide-brimmed hat, but there was something in the set of his jaw, the tension in his shoulders, that made Lena's pulse quicken.

For a moment, she stood still, unsure whether to approach or to retreat. She had seen this man before, at the edges of her father's conversations, in the margins of the dangerous world she'd spent most of her life ignoring. She wasn't the type to get tangled up in dangerous men, but this one felt different—darker, like the storm that was rolling in.

The bartender, a thick-set man with a weathered face, caught her eye and nodded toward the stranger.

"You looking for him?" The words were rough, as though they'd been dragged from the depths of a secret he wasn't sure he wanted to share.

Lena hesitated. "I'm not sure." She adjusted her stance, every muscle in her body tightening with anticipation. "But I'm looking for answers."

The bartender shrugged, a nonchalant gesture that spoke volumes. "He doesn't do small talk."

Lena took a slow breath, her eyes never leaving the man at the end of the bar. She had come this far, and there was no turning back now.

With purposeful steps, she moved toward him, her heels

clicking softly against the worn floorboards. As she approached, she noticed the way his posture stiffened, as if he had sensed her presence before she even spoke.

When she stopped beside him, she finally saw his face—strong, chiseled features, sharp angles, but with an underlying weariness in his dark eyes. His gaze flicked over her for a split second, cold and assessing, before it softened just enough to be unsettling.

"You're not the usual type to come into places like this," he said, his voice a low, gravelly rumble that made her skin prickle.

Lena's heart stuttered for just a moment, but she forced herself to meet his gaze, pushing aside the unease that bloomed in her chest. "I'm not here for usual things."

He raised an eyebrow, intrigued but wary. He took a sip of his drink, watching her over the rim of his glass, as if considering whether she was worth his time.

"I'm looking for someone," Lena said, her voice steady despite the tension swirling in her stomach. "Someone who might know about a family secret. Someone who has a lot of answers but doesn't share them freely."

The man set his glass down with deliberate slowness, his fingers lingering around the rim. "Sounds like you've been talking to the wrong people."

The words cut through the air like a knife. Lena felt the weight

The First Encounter

of his assessment, as though he had already sized her up in an instant. His eyes narrowed slightly, but there was a flicker of something beneath the surface—curiosity, perhaps, or wariness.

She leaned in, her pulse quickening as she lowered her voice. "I need to know everything. About my father. About what he was mixed up in."

For the first time, the man's expression shifted, a faint flicker of recognition in his eyes. But it was gone before she could fully decipher it.

"Your father," he said quietly, almost to himself, as if weighing the decision to engage further. "He was never the type to leave things behind easily."

Lena's chest tightened. "You know him?"

His lips twitched at the corner, a ghost of a smile that didn't quite reach his eyes. "I knew him. He was tangled up in things that most people wouldn't even begin to understand. And now, it looks like you're tangled up in it, too."

Lena didn't flinch. She had known this would come—this moment when the truth would break through like shards of glass. "So, you're the one who can help me?"

The man's gaze shifted slightly, and for a moment, there was a flicker of something—danger, or perhaps something darker. The way he studied her suggested that he was calculating, trying to figure out if she was truly worth the risk. But then he sighed, the sound low and resigned.

"You're already in this too deep," he murmured, almost as if to himself. "And so am I."

A chill ran down her spine, the weight of his words sinking in. She wasn't sure what he meant, but the subtle tension in his tone was enough to tell her that the answers she sought would come at a far greater cost than she was ready for.

The storm outside roared to life, and the first drops of rain began to hit the windows with an urgent rhythm, as if nature itself was preparing for something. Lena swallowed hard, her hand instinctively gripping the edge of the bar as she took a step closer.

"What do you know about my father?" she pressed, her voice quieter now, her determination hardening.

The man paused, his eyes flickering to the door, then back to her. For a split second, it felt as though he was about to say something—something that could change everything.

But instead, he took another drink, the glass emptying with a slow, deliberate motion.

"Everything you need to know, you already know," he said cryptically, his tone tinged with a knowing sadness. "But be careful, Lena. Some things are better left buried."

Before she could respond, the bartender's voice cut through the tension, louder now. "Better take your leave, sweetheart. He's not the kind you want to stick around for."

Lena's chest tightened. The weight of the man's gaze bore into her like a dark promise, but the words left her breathless. This was only the beginning.

Two

A Cold War

The rain came down in sheets, battering the windows of Lena's apartment as though nature itself was waging a war outside. The room was dimly lit, the only light coming from a single lamp on the far side, casting long shadows across the worn wooden floor. Lena stood by the window, staring out at the storm, her mind a whirlwind of thoughts and questions that wouldn't let her rest.

She couldn't shake the image of him—the man at the bar. His eyes, dark and unreadable, had lingered in her mind long after she left. There was something about him, something magnetic yet dangerous. The way his voice rumbled in the quiet of the bar, the way he seemed to hold all the answers but refused to give them away—Lena felt as though she had just brushed against the edge of something far larger than herself. And she was already in too deep.

A knock on the door interrupted her thoughts, sharp and insistent.

Lena's heart skipped a beat as she turned away from the window. She hadn't been expecting anyone. Her hand hovered over the doorknob for a moment, the air thick with tension. She knew it wasn't just anyone who would show up at her door uninvited, not in this city, not at this hour.

She opened the door cautiously, just wide enough to see the person standing on the other side.

It was him. The man from the bar.

For a moment, neither of them spoke. The silence stretched between them like a taut wire, both waiting for the other to make the first move. The storm raged behind him, the wind howling like a warning.

He stood there, his figure half-shrouded in the dark, his posture tense but not threatening. The dim hallway light glinted off the edges of his worn leather jacket, making it look as though he had stepped out of the shadows himself. His eyes met hers—those same dark eyes—and Lena felt a sharp jolt of recognition, though she had barely known him for more than a few minutes.

"What do you want?" she asked, her voice barely above a whisper, a mixture of curiosity and caution threading through her words.

He studied her, as though deciding whether to step inside or leave. His gaze flickered over her shoulder, his eyes scanning the room behind her before returning to her face. There was something in the way he looked at her—appraising, calculating, as though he were trying to piece her together, to figure out what made her tick.

"I thought you might want some answers," he said finally, his voice as low and gravelly as she remembered. There was an edge to it now, a trace of something darker beneath the surface. "But not here. Not like this."

Lena's pulse quickened. "What does that mean?"

He shifted slightly, leaning against the doorframe, his expression unreadable. "It means we need to talk somewhere more private. Somewhere you won't be able to eavesdrop on yourself."

Lena felt the hairs on the back of her neck stand up. It wasn't the first time someone had warned her about being too inquisitive, but this was different. This man wasn't just warning her—he was inviting her into something she wasn't sure she was ready for.

And yet, she found herself stepping aside, allowing him to enter.

The moment the door clicked shut behind them, the air in the room seemed to change. The weight of the unspoken hung between them like a thick fog, thick with tension. She motioned for him to sit, though she didn't follow him to the couch. Instead, she remained standing, her arms crossed over her chest as though trying to protect herself from something she couldn't quite name.

He took a seat without hesitation, leaning back with a casual ease that seemed out of place in the charged atmosphere.

For a long moment, neither of them spoke. The sound of the rain drummed against the windows, filling the silence, but it only seemed to deepen the tension.

"I didn't expect you to follow me," Lena said finally, breaking the silence. Her voice was steady, but the quickened beat of her heart betrayed her calm exterior.

He didn't flinch, didn't look surprised. His eyes remained fixed on hers. "You didn't expect me to come at all."

She couldn't deny that he was right. She had left the bar with every intention of moving on, of finding her own way. But something about him had drawn her back—something she couldn't explain. And now, here they were.

"Why are you really here?" Lena asked, her voice sharp now, as though she was trying to carve the truth out of him.

His lips curled into a faint, humorless smile. "You don't waste any time, do you?"

"Life's too short for games," she replied, her gaze never leaving his. "Either you tell me what you know, or you walk out that door and disappear. Just like everyone else."

The smile faded from his lips, and for a moment, his eyes darkened, the mask of indifference slipping just enough for Lena to see the faintest flicker of something else—something that felt like regret, or maybe caution.

"I'm not here to disappear, Lena," he said quietly. "I'm here because you're already in this. Whether you want to be or not."

Her heart skipped a beat at the way he said her name—low, deliberate, like he had known her for far longer than she cared to admit.

"Then tell me what you know," she pressed, taking a step closer. The storm outside seemed to draw closer, as though it were waiting for the revelation, hanging on the edge of the moment.

He exhaled sharply, his fingers drumming against the worn fabric of his jacket. His gaze flickered away from her, as though trying to weigh how much of the truth he was willing to reveal.

"The man you're looking for," he began slowly, his voice softer now, "he's not someone you want to find. Not unless you're prepared for what's coming."

Lena felt her throat tighten. "What's coming?"

His eyes locked onto hers again, and for a moment, the air between them felt charged with something she couldn't quite define. There was a warning in his gaze, but there was also something else—a depth, a vulnerability that didn't quite match the hardened exterior he showed the world.

"You think you're chasing answers," he said, his voice low and steady. "But what you're chasing is a storm. And once you're in it, there's no getting out."

She opened her mouth to respond, but the words caught in her throat. There was a finality to his tone, something that made her blood run cold. And yet, despite the warning, despite the chill in the room, Lena couldn't pull herself away.

"You're saying I should stop?" she asked, her voice quiet now, edged with the ghost of doubt.

He didn't answer right away, instead rising from his seat with a fluid movement that made the space between them feel suddenly smaller. He took a step toward her, his presence filling the room like a force she couldn't resist.

"No," he said quietly, his voice softer than before. "I'm saying that you don't have a choice. You're already too far in."

Lena's breath caught in her chest. She should have felt fear, should have turned him away, but instead, something inside her yearned to know more.

A shift passed between them, the air electric with the weight of unsaid words. She could feel it in her bones—the storm was just beginning. And whatever it was, it would change everything.

Three

The Spark Ignites

The storm had passed by when Lena stepped outside the next morning, but the air still carried the lingering scent of damp earth and fresh rain. She stood at the edge of the building, watching as droplets clung to the leaves, catching the light in a shimmering dance. Her mind, however, was elsewhere. It was difficult to focus on the beauty around her when the man from the bar was still at the forefront of her thoughts.

His words echoed in her mind like a haunting refrain: You're already too far in.

The truth of it clawed at her. She hadn't wanted to be drawn into this. She hadn't asked for the complications, the danger, and yet here she was—no closer to understanding the full scope of what her father had left behind and now wrapped up in the shadows of a man she barely knew. And yet, she couldn't shake the undeniable pull she felt whenever he was near.

Her phone buzzed in her pocket, breaking the momentary stillness, and she pulled it out without thinking. A message from an unlisted number flashed on the screen:

"Meet me tonight. Don't bring anyone. 9 p.m. The Docks."

Her heart thudded in her chest. She knew who it was from. The message was direct, sharp, the kind that demanded her compliance without explanation. It didn't surprise her, but it unsettled her all the same. She glanced at the time—5 p.m. The hours until then would drag by in agonizing suspense.

It was almost as if she could feel him now, even though she wasn't at the bar. The weight of his presence lingered on her skin, a shadow just beyond her reach. She didn't understand why she kept returning to him, why her body responded to him with such urgency. It was like a spark had been struck, and now there was no way to put out the fire that had started.

By the time night fell, the air had grown heavier again, thick with the promise of another storm. Lena's footsteps echoed down the alleyway leading toward the docks, her heart beating a steady rhythm of anticipation and dread. The city seemed quieter now, the usual hum of life dampened by the weather. Only the occasional hiss of a distant car tire breaking through puddles broke the stillness.

The Docks were as desolate as she had remembered. Cold,

concrete structures loomed over the water, and the smell of saltwater mixed with the lingering scent of fish and rust. It was the kind of place where secrets lived, buried beneath the grime and the decay of the city's underbelly. And it was where everything seemed to converge for her.

Lena's breath misted in the cool night air as she approached the meeting point—the old shipping warehouse near the end of Pier 7. She had no idea what to expect, but every fiber of her being screamed that this was it, that tonight would be the night everything changed.

Her footsteps faltered as she reached the entrance. The door was slightly ajar, and from within, she could hear the low hum of music—soft jazz, its melancholic notes floating through the cracked walls. There was a warmth to it, a stark contrast to the chill of the night, but it did nothing to soothe the tension in her chest.

She stepped inside, her heels clicking sharply against the wooden floor. The interior was dimly lit, shadows creeping over the rows of crates and abandoned equipment. A single light hung above the bar area in the corner, casting long, angled beams that barely illuminated the space. And there he was—standing by the bar, his back to her, a drink in hand.

He hadn't noticed her approach, but the moment she stepped further into the room, his posture shifted. He straightened, turned slowly, and his eyes met hers. There was no surprise, no question in his gaze. It was the same look he'd given her at the bar—the one that made her feel as if he could see straight through her, as if he knew everything before she even spoke.

"You came," he said, his voice low and smooth, like the roll of thunder before a storm.

Lena didn't answer right away. Instead, she walked toward him, her steps slow and deliberate, as if the closer she got, the more her mind could reconcile what she was doing. The room felt smaller now, the air thicker with each step she took toward him. There was something about the way he stood—his eyes never leaving hers—that made the space between them feel electric, charged with a current that neither of them could ignore.

"I came," she replied, her voice steady but laced with an edge she couldn't quite hide. "Now, tell me why I'm here."

He studied her for a long moment, his gaze intense and unreadable. For a second, it almost felt as though he was weighing her, measuring how far she was willing to go. Then, without a word, he gestured toward the empty chair beside him. The invitation was clear.

She sat, her movements measured, as though she was afraid that the wrong move would tip everything off balance. But despite the caution in her posture, there was an undeniable pulse of something else—something that pushed her closer to him. Something that made her blood run hot and her thoughts scatter.

"I know what you're looking for," he said, his tone quiet, almost conspiratorial. "And I know why you're looking for it."

Lena's breath caught in her throat. She leaned forward, her eyes narrowing slightly. "Do you?"

His lips curled into a faint, knowing smile. "I do. And I'm telling you, it's not going to be easy to find."

She hesitated for a beat before speaking again. "Why don't you just tell me then? All of it. What's the point of playing these games?"

He tilted his head, studying her for a moment before his smile faded. His eyes darkened, and the mood in the room shifted instantly. There was a heaviness to the air now, thick with an unspoken truth, a kind of warning she couldn't ignore.

"It's not a game, Lena," he said, his voice dropping lower, a dangerous edge creeping in. "It's a fire. And once it's lit, there's no putting it out."

Lena felt a shiver run through her, but she refused to let it show. "What do you mean?"

He stood, pacing away from her for a moment, as if to collect his thoughts—or perhaps to give her space to absorb what he was saying. His movements were fluid, precise, like a predator circling its prey, only he wasn't the one hunting. She was.

"I'm not the one you should be afraid of," he said, his voice low. "But I can promise you this—if you keep digging, if you keep chasing the answers to your father's secrets, you'll find yourself in a firestorm. And once you're in, there's no escape. You'll

The Spark Ignites

either burn, or you'll learn to survive."

The words hung in the air, heavy and foreboding. Lena swallowed, trying to steady the thudding of her heart. She wasn't sure what frightened her more—the threat in his voice or the part of her that wanted to believe him. Part of her wanted to back away, to leave this all behind, but something kept her rooted in place. Something she couldn't explain.

He turned back to her, his expression unreadable, but there was something softer in his gaze now, something like regret or guilt—though it was gone as quickly as it came. "You've already crossed a line, Lena," he said, his voice gentler this time. "And now, there's no going back."

Lena's mind raced, her body tensed. Every instinct told her to walk away, to turn around and leave before it was too late. But the fire inside her—the one that had been sparked the moment she laid eyes on him—refused to be extinguished.

"So what now?" she asked, her voice steady, but her breath shaky with the weight of everything that hung between them.

His eyes softened, and for the briefest of moments, she saw something else in them—a flicker of something human, something real. But just as quickly, the mask returned, and the distance between them seemed to grow once more.

"We wait," he said simply. "And when the time comes, you'll know what to do."

Four

Secrets Unveiled

The chill of the night air bit at Lena's skin as she stood at the edge of the docks, watching the last remnants of the storm pass over the horizon. The clouds had broken apart, leaving streaks of pale moonlight to spill across the water, casting everything in a silvery haze. For a moment, everything felt still, as if the world were holding its breath—waiting for something to happen, for something to be revealed.

Lena's pulse had yet to settle after her meeting with him. The man with the dark eyes and the quiet menace. Damian. His name lingered on her lips like a forbidden thought. She had left the warehouse with more questions than answers, her mind churning with everything he had said—and everything he hadn't.

"If you keep chasing the answers, you'll find yourself in a

firestorm." His words replayed over and over in her mind, as sharp and dangerous as shards of glass.

She'd known the moment she stepped into this mess that there would be consequences. But she hadn't expected the weight of it to feel so real, so suffocating. The closer she got to the truth about her father's life—and death—the more she felt the shadows closing in on her.

The message from the previous night had been brief, but it had been clear enough: Meet me tomorrow. The usual place. Don't bring anyone.

She had been wary, but there was no turning back now. If there was a shred of truth in what Damian had told her, if he really had the answers she needed, then she couldn't afford to be cautious. Not anymore.

The evening had drawn on, and as dusk settled in, Lena found herself once again in front of the old building. The air had a sharpness to it now, the kind that came with late autumn nights. She could feel the tension building with every step, the weight of it settling heavily in her chest. There was no one else on the streets, only the sound of distant waves lapping against the shore and the occasional gust of wind that seemed to push her forward, urging her toward the unknown.

She reached the door, the same worn, wooden entrance that she had passed through just a day before. Her heart was pounding now, not just from the fear of the unknown, but from the strange magnetism she felt toward him. Toward Damian. The way his presence had affected her from the moment they met, how his voice still echoed in her mind, how his gaze had felt like a thousand secrets wrapped into one. There was something about him—something she didn't trust, but couldn't stay away from.

The door creaked open, and the familiar scent of whiskey, cigar smoke, and saltwater filled the air. The low hum of jazz music drifted from the corner of the room, its melancholic notes hanging in the air like a memory. The bar was quiet, far emptier than it had been the previous night, but Lena's eyes immediately found him. He was sitting at the same spot, the same brooding figure in the dim light, his body turned slightly away from her but his eyes already trained on the door as she entered.

She froze for just a moment, her breath catching in her throat. There was something different about him tonight—something that felt more urgent, more serious. She had seen the dark side of him before, the part that spoke with authority and made her feel like she was standing on the edge of something she didn't fully understand. But tonight, there was a vulnerability in his gaze that she hadn't noticed before. It was fleeting, but it was enough to make her pause.

She walked toward him, her footsteps steady but her heart racing. She didn't know what was waiting for her tonight—whether it would be another cryptic warning, or something more. The closer she got to him, the more the world seemed to narrow, until all that existed was the space between them. He hadn't moved, hadn't spoken, but his presence was overwhelming, suffocating in its own way.

She stopped a few feet away from him, her eyes meeting his. There was no greeting this time, no casual banter. Just the weight of unspoken understanding.

"You came," he said softly, his voice barely above a whisper. But there was something in his tone, something like relief, or maybe regret—something she couldn't quite place.

Lena didn't answer immediately. She simply nodded, taking a step closer. Her senses seemed to heighten in his presence. The sound of her breath felt louder, the warmth of his body close enough that she could feel the faint heat radiating off him.

"Tell me what you know," she said, her voice steadier than she felt. "Tell me everything."

He didn't answer right away, and Lena wondered if he even intended to. He simply studied her, his gaze sharp, like a predator sizing up its prey. It was unsettling how easily he seemed to read her, how well he knew the questions she hadn't yet asked. There was a part of her that wanted to turn away, that wanted to run from whatever this was, but she couldn't. She was too far in now, tangled in a web that she hadn't even realized she was caught in.

"I know what you're looking for," Damian finally said, his voice dark, almost regretful. "And I know the cost."

Lena swallowed, her mouth dry. "What cost?"

He exhaled sharply, his hand reaching for the glass of whiskey in front of him. He lifted it slowly, eyes never leaving her, as if savoring the moment, savoring her tension. "Everything, Lena. You'll lose more than you expect. The closer you get to the truth, the more you'll lose. People don't just disappear for no reason. And your father... he was tangled up in something far bigger than you realize."

Her chest tightened, the breath leaving her lungs in a sharp rush. She wasn't sure if it was fear or something else—something like anger or betrayal. The pieces of the puzzle were starting to fit together, but they didn't form the picture she had hoped for. They were jagged, broken fragments that didn't make sense.

"My father's dead," she said quietly, her voice thick with emotion. "How could he be involved in something—something that dangerous?"

Damian's eyes softened, just a little, and the brief flash of vulnerability returned. "Because your father wasn't who you think he was. He was part of something that goes beyond you, beyond all of us."

Lena felt a lump rise in her throat. The world she had built around herself, the life she had known, suddenly felt so small, so fragile. Everything she thought she knew about her father, about the family she came from, was unraveling before her eyes. And as much as she wanted to stop the process, to push him away and pretend this wasn't happening, she couldn't.

"Why are you telling me this?" she asked, her voice barely above a whisper. "What do you want from me?"

Damian's gaze shifted, his lips curling into a faint, sad smile. "I don't want anything from you, Lena. I'm just trying to make sure you don't lose yourself in this."

His words hung in the air between them, heavy with meaning, and Lena's heart began to race once more. She wanted to believe him, wanted to trust him, but the truth felt like a jagged knife pressing against her ribs. She could feel the tension, the crackling energy between them—familiar, yet foreign. She could taste the danger in the air, feel it clinging to her skin like smoke.

And yet, there was something else beneath it all, something warm, something that stirred in her chest when he looked at her. It wasn't just fear or curiosity anymore. There was something more, something deeper. She didn't know if she was ready for it, but she knew she wouldn't be able to turn away.

"Tell me what you know," she said again, her voice low and resolute. "I'm ready."

Damian didn't move for a moment, his eyes never leaving hers. Then, slowly, he set the glass down and leaned in closer, his voice dropping to a whisper.

"Your father was the key to all of this. And now, it's your turn to finish what he started."

Lena's breath caught in her throat. The spark that had been smoldering inside her flared into a flame.

And she realized, for better or worse, there was no going back.

Five

Crossed Wires

The morning light filtered weakly through the blinds of Lena's apartment, casting long, angular shadows across the room. The air was still thick with the remnants of the storm from the night before, the weight of it lingering in the heavy silence that had settled over her. Lena sat at the kitchen table, her fingers absentmindedly tracing the rim of her coffee cup, the warmth of the liquid in stark contrast to the coldness that had taken root inside her. She had hoped that sleep would bring some clarity, but instead, her mind had spiraled through the conversations from the night before, each word, each glance, gnawing at her like an itch she couldn't scratch.

Damian's face lingered in her thoughts—his voice, calm and assured, his eyes dark and unreadable. "Everything you thought you knew is a lie." His words echoed through her mind like a drumbeat, relentless and unforgiving. The more she thought about what he had said, the more the edges of the truth blurred into something she wasn't sure she was ready to confront.

She couldn't deny the pull she felt toward him, the way his presence seemed to wrap around her like a shadow. But every time she let herself get too close to that feeling, something inside her recoiled. She had learned the hard way that trust was a currency that could buy nothing in the world she now found herself in. The man who had died—her father—had left behind a legacy of lies, and Damian had been the one to reveal that to her. Whether she liked it or not, the puzzle pieces were falling into place, and every answer she uncovered only raised more questions.

A sharp knock at the door startled her, and she jumped, spilling some of her coffee onto the table. She cursed under her breath, quickly grabbing a napkin to wipe it up. Whoever it was could have been a number of people, but the unease she felt in the pit of her stomach told her exactly who it was. She wasn't surprised when she opened the door to find him standing there.

Damian.

The weight of his presence filled the doorway as soon as he entered, his tall, broad frame blocking the little light that filtered into the hallway. He was dressed in the same dark leather jacket from the night before, his hair slightly damp from the morning mist. There was a tension about him, an electricity that seemed to hum in the air around him, but his expression was unreadable—an impenetrable mask that told her nothing of what he was thinking.

"Damian," Lena said, her voice steady, though the knot in her stomach tightened at the sight of him. "What are you doing here?"

His eyes scanned the apartment with an almost predatory gaze, taking in every detail before meeting her eyes once more. "We need to talk," he said, his voice low, edged with urgency. "Now."

Lena hesitated, a cold shiver running down her spine. "I'm not sure I want to know more, Damian. Not after what you said last night."

His jaw tightened, the only sign of emotion breaking through his carefully controlled exterior. "You don't have a choice, Lena," he said, his tone now hard and insistent. "There are things you need to understand before it's too late."

Before she could respond, he pushed past her, stepping into the apartment without waiting for her permission. The door clicked shut behind him, and Lena's heart rate spiked. Something was off. There was a subtle, but undeniable change in the air between them. He had come for a reason, but she couldn't figure out what it was just yet.

"Sit down," he said, gesturing toward the couch, his eyes still fixed on her with that same unreadable intensity. "We don't have much time."

Lena stood frozen in the doorway for a moment, torn between instinct and curiosity. She wasn't used to feeling this unsettled. It was more than just the way he made her feel—it was the weight of the situation. The game had shifted, and she wasn't sure whether she was ready for it to escalate.

Reluctantly, she sat across from him, her fingers twisting nervously around the hem of her sleeve. "What's going on?" she asked, her voice quieter than she meant it to be.

Damian didn't answer right away. Instead, he reached into the inside pocket of his jacket, pulling out a small, crumpled envelope. He slid it across the table toward her, his fingers brushing hers as he did so. The contact was brief, but it left a spark in its wake—one that made her pulse quicken and her breath catch in her throat. She couldn't afford to focus on that. Not now.

Lena opened the envelope with trembling fingers. Inside was a photograph—grainy, black and white, but unmistakable. Her father, standing in front of a building she didn't recognize, his face set in an expression she had never seen before—one of quiet determination, but also something else. Fear. A sense of urgency that she couldn't quite place.

"What is this?" she asked, her voice a whisper as she traced her fingers over the image. The building behind him was an old warehouse, crumbling at the edges, and there were people gathered in the background—figures she couldn't make out, but they looked familiar in some way.

"Your father wasn't just involved in shady deals, Lena," Damian said, his voice taking on a grim edge. "He was part of something much bigger. Something dangerous."

Lena's mind raced. The photograph was one of many she hadn't seen before—one that painted a picture of her father she didn't know existed. She felt the ground beneath her shift. What had her father been involved in?

"You're not telling me everything," Lena said, her eyes narrowing as she looked at him. "You're hiding something."

Damian didn't flinch. His gaze remained steady, almost unreadable. "I'm telling you everything I can. But there are some things… some people you're not ready to face yet."

Lena's pulse thudded in her ears as she sat back in her seat. "What aren't you telling me, Damian?"

He leaned forward, his face softening for just a moment. "I'm trying to protect you, Lena. From all of this."

She swallowed hard, her voice barely audible. "Protect me? From what?"

He didn't answer right away, and for a moment, Lena wondered if he would ever speak the truth she so desperately needed. Finally, he exhaled sharply, his gaze flickering to the window. "From the people who killed your father."

Her breath caught in her throat. The room seemed to tilt, the walls pressing in on her as the words landed like a hammer strike.

"The people who—what?" She could barely form the words, her

mind reeling. "You're saying he didn't die of natural causes?"

Damian's silence was answer enough.

She could feel the air around them crackling with tension now, thick and suffocating. Lena's heart raced as everything she thought she knew about her father, her family, her life, began to unravel. And there, in the middle of it all, was Damian—a man she barely knew, but who seemed to hold the key to the dark secrets she had never wanted to uncover.

Her gaze snapped back to him. "Why are you here, Damian? Why are you telling me this?"

He studied her for a long moment, as if weighing whether to reveal more. His lips parted slightly, but before he could speak, the sharp sound of footsteps echoed outside the door.

Someone was coming.

Damian's eyes hardened instantly, his body going still. "We need to leave. Now."

The urgency in his voice sliced through the fog of confusion that had settled in her mind. She didn't hesitate. The room seemed to close in on them as she grabbed her coat and followed him out into the hallway, her heart hammering in her chest.

As they moved swiftly down the stairwell, Lena couldn't shake the feeling that the world had just shifted beneath her feet—and this time, there was no going back.

Six

Firestorm

The rain had returned, falling in heavy, unrelenting sheets that blurred the skyline into a haze of gray and black. Lena stood at the edge of the alley, her coat pulled tight around her, and her collar turned up to shield her from the downpour. The city was muffled by the storm, the usual sounds of life drowned by the torrential rain. But in the silence, there was something else—something in the air that crackled with an electric charge, as though the world itself was holding its breath, waiting for the inevitable.

Lena's heart thudded in her chest, her hands clenched tightly around the strap of her bag as she looked down the dark alley. She had followed Damian's instructions without question, stepping into the night with nothing but uncertainty and a burning need for answers. But as the minutes ticked by, she felt a growing unease gnaw at her.

Where was he?

She glanced around, her eyes darting nervously. The alley was empty, save for the faint glow of a streetlamp at the far end and the ever-present shadows that seemed to stretch and twist with each gust of wind. The world felt far too quiet, the heavy rain muffling everything but the beat of her own pulse. Her stomach churned, a sense of foreboding wrapping itself around her, as if she were waiting for something—or someone—to break through the silence.

A soft step behind her broke the stillness, and Lena froze. She didn't have to turn around to know who it was.

Damian.

His presence was unmistakable, a weight in the air that she could feel without even looking. Her breath hitched in her throat as he stepped into her line of sight, his figure emerging from the shadows like a phantom, his dark coat soaked through from the rain. His eyes met hers, dark and unreadable, and for a brief moment, the world seemed to narrow to just the two of them, standing there in the pouring rain, caught in a moment that felt like it was suspended in time.

"You came," he said, his voice low and calm, a hint of something unreadable in the way he said it. There was no surprise in his tone—just a quiet acknowledgment, as if he had known she would be here.

Lena nodded, though she wasn't sure what she was agreeing to.

She didn't trust him, not completely. But the pull he had over her was undeniable, like a magnet that she couldn't break free from, no matter how hard she tried.

"You said we needed to leave," she said, her voice tight with suspicion. "What's going on?"

Damian glanced around, his gaze sharp, as if he were assessing their surroundings, weighing something only he could see. His jaw tightened, the muscles in his face flickering with tension. "We've overstayed our welcome," he muttered, his voice lower now, laced with urgency. "They're coming for you."

Lena's heart skipped a beat. "Who?"

"The people who killed your father," Damian said quietly, his eyes never leaving hers. "The ones who've been pulling the strings. They know you're looking for answers, and they won't stop until they've erased every trace of your father's past."

Lena's blood ran cold at his words. She had known, deep down, that this was more than just a few unanswered questions about her father's life. But hearing it spoken out loud—hearing Damian say it in such a calm, collected way—made the danger feel more real, more immediate.

"How do you know this?" she asked, her voice barely above a whisper.

Damian didn't answer right away. Instead, he stepped closer, his eyes scanning the alley once more. The tension in the air was thick, like the calm before a storm, and Lena could feel the weight of it pressing in on her. She could hear her breath in her ears, steady but quick, as her heart raced.

"They're already here," he said suddenly, his voice low and urgent. "We need to move. Now."

Before Lena could respond, the sound of footsteps echoed in the distance, sharp and deliberate. The hair on the back of her neck stood on end, and her pulse quickened. She turned, her eyes straining to pierce the darkness, to see where the threat was coming from.

Damian's hand shot out, grabbing her wrist with surprising force, pulling her into the shadows before she could even think. The sudden movement caught her off guard, and for a moment, she stumbled, her heart pounding in her chest as her body collided with his.

His grip tightened on her wrist, steady and unyielding. "Stay quiet," he murmured, his voice urgent, his breath warm against her ear. The sensation of his proximity sent a jolt of something electric through her, but she forced herself to focus, to listen. The footsteps were closer now, echoing louder as they approached.

Lena pressed herself against the wall, her back flush against the cold stone, her breath shallow as she tried to steady herself. Damian stood just a few inches away, his body so close that she could feel the heat radiating off him, his presence overwhelming and protective. The tension between them was palpable, but there was no time to acknowledge it—not now, not with the threat so close.

The footsteps grew louder, and Lena's heart hammered in her chest. She could feel the weight of the moment pressing down on her. Every instinct told her to run, to get out of there, but she knew it was too late. They were already here, and there was nowhere to hide.

Damian's grip on her wrist tightened, and for the briefest moment, their eyes locked. His gaze was fierce, intense—darker than it had been before, as if something inside him had shifted. Something primal. Something dangerous.

"Don't make a sound," he whispered, his voice a low command.

Lena's breath caught in her throat as she nodded, her chest tight with fear. Her body was still pressed against his, and she could feel his every movement, every shift, as if he were trying to shield her from the world outside. The intimacy of it—of being so close to him in the dark, in the rain—made her heart race for reasons she didn't fully understand. There was a part of her that wanted to lean into the warmth of him, to let him take control, to let him shield her from whatever was coming. But she couldn't let herself forget the truth—he wasn't here to protect her. He was here because their fates were tied together by something far more dangerous than either of them could escape.

The footsteps drew closer, and Lena's breath caught in her throat. She could hear the soft rustle of fabric, the faint clink of something metallic. They were armed. They were here for her.

Damian's eyes flickered to the end of the alley, his body tense, every muscle coiled as if ready to spring into action. He didn't make a sound, didn't give any indication that he was about to move, but Lena could feel the shift in the air—the charged energy that came with the quiet before the storm.

Then, just as suddenly as it had appeared, the sound of footsteps stopped. A figure emerged from the shadows, and Lena's stomach twisted.

It was a man, tall and broad-shouldered, his face hidden beneath a hood. He paused at the mouth of the alley, scanning the street, his eyes flicking from side to side as though searching for something—or someone.

Lena's breath hitched, and her pulse hammered in her ears as Damian's grip on her wrist loosened just enough for her to breathe. His eyes never left the man, his body a perfect blend of stillness and readiness. He was waiting. Waiting for the perfect moment.

And then, without warning, the man stepped forward, his hand brushing against the wall as he moved deeper into the alley. Damian's arm shot out, pulling Lena closer into the shadows, his body a solid barrier between her and the man. The world seemed to hold its breath.

The storm raged on, but all Lena could hear was the beating of her own heart—loud, chaotic, as the world around her threatened to explode.

Seven

Torn Between Desire and Duty

The morning after the narrow escape from the alley was no less heavy than the night before. The storm had subsided, leaving behind a thick, oppressive fog that hung in the air, clinging to the streets like a memory that refused to fade. The city seemed quieter, as though the previous night's events had stilled everything around it, as if the earth itself was holding its breath. But for Lena, the weight of the world pressed on her chest, and each step she took was heavier than the last.

She hadn't asked Damian what had happened after the man had appeared at the mouth of the alley. She hadn't needed to. They had moved quickly, silently, back to his car—a black sedan that seemed to blend with the shadows—and then he'd driven her to the only place that felt safe in that moment: a small, nondescript apartment hidden in the maze of the city's old district. The place smelled faintly of dust, and the floor creaked underfoot with each step. It was hardly a sanctuary, but it was where she would stay for now.

Lena stood by the window, staring out at the city below. The view wasn't much—just a stretch of rooftops and distant towers veiled by the lingering fog—but it offered her a moment of clarity, a brief respite from the chaos swirling around her. The image of the hooded man still burned in her mind, his presence like an itch she couldn't scratch. Who was he? Why had he been following her? And why had Damian's grip on her wrist tightened so urgently when he'd seen him?

Her reflection in the window stared back at her, pale and drawn. Her hair, once neatly combed, hung loose around her shoulders, a stark contrast to the tightness in her chest. The more she thought about the events of the past twenty-four hours, the more the gnawing feeling in her gut grew. Damian had been her savior, her protector. But every moment with him felt like walking on a knife's edge. She wasn't sure whether he was guiding her toward the truth—or leading her deeper into the dark.

There was a knock at the door, a low, insistent rapping that jolted her from her thoughts. Her heart skipped a beat as she turned toward the sound, and instinctively, she walked to the door, every step heavy with the knowledge that whatever was about to unfold would change everything.

She hesitated for a moment before opening it, and there he stood—Damian. His figure filled the doorway, tall and imposing, his coat soaked from the rain outside, but his eyes were the only thing that seemed untouched by the storm. He stared at her with that same unreadable intensity, but there was something more—something raw, something unspoken that hung between them.

Lena's breath caught in her throat, and she stepped back, allowing him to enter without a word. The space between them was charged, thick with tension. She could feel the pull of him, a magnetism that was impossible to ignore. It was a quiet storm in itself—one she couldn't seem to escape.

"Are you alright?" Damian's voice was soft, but there was a note of concern beneath it that caught her off guard.

She nodded, though she wasn't sure it was true. "I'm fine," she said, but the lie tasted bitter on her tongue. She wasn't fine—not by a long shot. Every part of her ached with the need for answers, but there was a nagging fear in the back of her mind, one she couldn't shake.

Damian stepped into the apartment, closing the door behind him with a soft click. He stood there for a moment, just looking at her, his expression unreadable. His presence filled the room, and Lena felt it deep in her chest—his gravity, pulling her closer, making her feel both safe and vulnerable at the same time. He was the only constant in this whirlwind of confusion, yet she didn't know if she could trust him fully.

She had to ask the question. She had to get the truth out of him.

"What happened last night?" Lena's voice was steady, but the words were sharp, edged with the urgency she felt. "Who was that man in the alley? Why did you react like that?"

Damian's eyes flickered, the only sign that the question had struck a nerve. He exhaled slowly, the sound almost imperceptible, before he spoke, his voice low and measured.

"You're not safe here," he said, the words cutting through the air like a blade. "You have to understand, Lena, the people who are after you—they won't stop. They don't care about who you are, only what you represent. Your father's death wasn't an accident. It was a warning."

Lena's stomach dropped. The words were like poison, seeping into her veins, spreading cold and dark through her. "What do you mean? Who would want to kill my father? And why do they want me?"

Damian's gaze softened, just slightly, but the tension in his shoulders never eased. "Because your father was a part of something much bigger than anyone realized. Something that's been hidden for years. And you…" He paused, his eyes flickering with something unreadable, before continuing. "You're the key to unlocking it. The key to everything."

The words hung in the air, heavy and suffocating. Lena's heart raced as she processed what he'd just said. Her father—her father had been involved in something so dangerous that it had gotten him killed. And now, she was being dragged into it, whether she wanted to be or not.

"And what about you?" she asked, her voice quiet but steady. "Why are you helping me? What do you want from me?"

Damian took a step forward, his eyes never leaving hers. The distance between them seemed to shrink with each second that passed, until it felt as though the space between them was just a breath, a heartbeat. "I'm not asking for anything," he said softly. "I'm just trying to protect you from what's coming. From what I've already lost."

Lena's breath caught in her throat, her pulse quickening at the raw vulnerability in his voice. She had always seen him as the strong, silent type—the protector, the guide—but in that moment, she saw something else. There was pain in his eyes, something deeper than she had realized. And despite all the secrets he was keeping, despite the walls he had built around himself, she could see that he was just as trapped in this web as she was.

"I don't know what to do," she admitted, her voice barely above a whisper. "I don't know what I'm supposed to believe."

Damian's eyes softened, a flicker of something in his gaze that made her heart ache. He reached out, his hand brushing against hers, and the contact sent a shock of heat through her, sharp and sudden. It was like a spark in the dark, lighting something inside her that she wasn't sure she was ready to confront.

"You don't have to do this alone," he said, his voice low and steady. "I'll help you, Lena. But you have to trust me. You have to trust that I'm doing everything I can to keep you safe."

Lena's mind raced as she looked into his eyes, searching for any sign of deception, but all she saw was sincerity—and something else. Something she couldn't quite name, but that made her feel both terrified and alive all at once. The pull between them was undeniable, but the questions, the doubts, still swirled in her mind. Could she trust him? Could she trust the dangerous man who had been leading her deeper into a world of secrets and lies?

She wanted to believe him. She wanted to believe that he was trying to protect her. But the more she let herself believe, the more the fear grew—the fear that by trusting him, she was sealing her own fate.

"I don't know if I can," she said, her voice barely above a whisper. "I don't know if I can trust anyone."

Damian's hand remained on hers, steady and warm, and for a moment, she felt the weight of everything she had just said—and everything she hadn't said—press down on her.

"You don't have to trust anyone but yourself," he replied softly. "But you need to make a choice, Lena. A choice that could change everything."

Lena's heart raced as the weight of his words sank in. Her future, her past, everything she thought she knew, was suddenly unraveling before her eyes. And as she stood there, hand in his, she realized that the choice wasn't just about trust. It was about survival.

And whatever choice she made, there would be no turning back.

Eight

In the Eye of the Storm

The night air was thick with the scent of saltwater, mingling with the bitter edge of damp concrete as Lena walked through the deserted streets toward the dockside warehouse. The fog had settled heavily over the city again, swirling around her like a ghost that refused to leave. Each step she took seemed to push her further into a world that no longer felt safe, a world where the lines between friend and foe had blurred into something far more dangerous.

Her thoughts spun in frantic circles as she approached the edge of the pier. Every streetlight she passed flickered dimly, casting long, distorted shadows across the alleyways. The oppressive silence was broken only by the rhythmic creaking of the wooden planks beneath her boots and the occasional distant sound of a wave crashing against the shore. Everything about this place felt wrong—wrong in a way that made her skin crawl, the deep, gnawing sense that she had stepped too far into the unknown.

Damian had insisted they meet here, at the old warehouse by the docks, a place where the past and present seemed to collide in the rusting remnants of old shipping containers and derelict buildings. He hadn't given her many details, just a brief message to tell her it was time—time to face whatever awaited them, time to confront the hidden truths that had been eating away at everything she thought she knew about her life.

She had tried to fight the fear growing in her chest. After everything that had happened—after the man in the alley, after the dark revelations about her father's death—it was becoming clear that there was no way out of this. This was the path, and it led only one way: forward.

She paused at the entrance to the warehouse, her breath coming in shallow gasps as the fog swirled around her, clinging to her clothes and skin like a second layer. The place looked abandoned, its windows dark and covered in grime, the faded remnants of old signs barely visible through the mist. The large metal doors stood ajar, and a soft, rhythmic sound came from within—footsteps, low voices murmuring in the shadows, the sound of metal on metal.

Her heart clenched as she stepped inside, the door creaking softly behind her. The inside of the warehouse was cold, far colder than the outside air, the walls lined with old crates and barrels that hadn't seen use in years. The faint smell of oil and decay lingered in the air, a reminder of how forgotten this place had become. But tonight, it was far from abandoned.

Lena's gaze swept over the dimly lit interior, her eyes adjusting to the darkness. In the far corner, she saw him. Damian. His silhouette was outlined against a dull light, and as he turned to face her, his eyes caught hers with that same unyielding intensity that always made her feel as though he could see straight through her.

For a moment, they just stood there, facing each other across the expanse of the warehouse, as the space between them stretched thin with unsaid words. The tension was palpable, and the air between them seemed charged, like the calm before a storm. His posture was tense, but there was something different about him tonight. A weight in his gaze that hadn't been there before, something deeper that she couldn't quite place.

"You came," Damian said, his voice soft but edged with something that made her stomach tighten. His eyes flickered to the shadows around them before returning to her face.

"I don't know what's going on," Lena admitted, her voice steady despite the storm of emotions swirling inside her. "But I'm here. I need to know the truth. I need to know what you're hiding."

Damian didn't answer immediately. Instead, he took a step forward, his eyes scanning the room as though assessing some unseen danger. The room seemed to close in on them, the walls pressing in as the faint hum of voices grew louder, more distinct. It was a sound that made her senses prick with suspicion, an undercurrent of something darker, something she hadn't fully anticipated.

"This isn't the place for answers," Damian said quietly, his voice rough with something close to regret. "The truth you're looking for... it's bigger than you think."

Lena took a deep breath, forcing herself to stay calm even as the pressure inside her chest grew. "What do you mean?" she asked, stepping closer. "What's happening? Why are you hiding from me?"

Damian's jaw clenched, his eyes hardening. "I'm not hiding from you, Lena. I'm trying to protect you from the truth."

His words hit her like a punch to the gut. "From the truth? Or from what happens if I find out?"

For a brief moment, the anger in her voice caught him off guard, his eyes flickering with something close to surprise. But it was only for a second, quickly masked by the familiar coldness that had begun to settle between them. He took another step toward her, closing the distance between them, and Lena felt the air shift, the weight of his presence overwhelming her senses.

"You don't understand," he said, his voice barely above a whisper. "This isn't just about your father. It's about everything that's happening right now. There's a war, Lena. A war that's been brewing for years, and your father—he was at the center of it."

Lena's mind raced. A war? Her father had been a part of something far bigger than she could have ever imagined. A chill ran through her as the implications of his words sank in, and she shook her head, trying to push the panic down.

"Why me?" she asked, her voice trembling despite her best efforts. "Why am I being pulled into this? What does this have to do with me?"

Damian's eyes softened for a moment, the hardness in his gaze giving way to something else—something fragile. "Because you're the only one who can stop it. Your father knew it. And now, it's your turn to finish what he started."

Lena swallowed hard, her throat dry, her pulse quickening as the weight of his words pressed down on her. She had known, on some level, that this would be the answer, that she wasn't just chasing shadows. But hearing him say it—hearing him say it with such finality—made it all feel far too real.

Before she could respond, a loud crash echoed through the warehouse, followed by the sound of multiple footsteps—footsteps that weren't theirs. Someone else was here. Someone had followed them.

Lena's heart skipped a beat, and she instinctively took a step back, her hand reaching out to grip the edge of a nearby crate for support. Damian's eyes flashed toward the source of the sound, his body coiling with readiness. Without another word, he grabbed her arm, pulling her into the shadows just as figures emerged from the darkness.

They were everywhere. Shadows moved, sleek and dangerous, their faces hidden behind masks. The air seemed to vibrate with an oppressive sense of dread, and Lena could feel her breath catching in her chest as the realization hit her. This was the storm. The one they had been preparing for.

"Stay close," Damian murmured, his voice low, like the growl of a predator about to strike. His hand remained firm around her wrist as he led her deeper into the shadows, away from the approaching figures.

The men in masks were getting closer, their movements fluid and silent, but Lena could feel the weight of their presence, the danger they brought with them. She had no choice but to follow Damian as he moved, swift and quiet, his body close enough that she could feel the heat of him in the dark, his breath steady against her skin.

They ducked behind a stack of crates just as the masked figures closed in, their voices low and indistinct. Lena's heart pounded in her chest, the adrenaline flooding her veins as she pressed herself against Damian, every sense focused on the danger that loomed just beyond the darkness. She could feel him—feel the tension in his body as he held her close, his fingers tight around her wrist.

She didn't know how long they stayed like that, crouched in the darkness, the air thick with tension and fear. But every moment that passed made her more certain of one thing—there was no going back from this.

Whatever happened next, it was only the beginning.

Nine

A Heart's Reckoning

The night had never felt so cold.

Lena's fingers trembled as she wrapped her arms around herself, huddling into the corner of the small room they had taken refuge in. The walls seemed to close in around her, the air thick with the scent of mildew and damp wood, making it hard to breathe. The only light came from a single, flickering bulb overhead, casting long shadows that made the space feel claustrophobic, suffocating. Outside, the wind howled through the narrow alleyways, a distant, mournful sound that mirrored the turmoil inside her.

She hadn't expected to be here—not like this. Not with Damian, not after the storm that had surged between them. The warehouse had been the first battleground, but this—this felt like the aftermath of something far more dangerous. The stillness of the room held the tension of something unresolved, something about to break.

She could feel Damian's presence even before she turned to face him. He stood by the door, his body leaning against the frame, his arms crossed over his chest. His silhouette was a dark shadow against the dim light, his jaw set in a hard line, his face unreadable. The moment he had led her away from the warehouse—away from the masked figures who had nearly caught them both—he had turned into something else. Something distant.

Her gaze lingered on him, her heart racing with a mixture of confusion and something deeper—something she couldn't quite name. She had been swept up in the madness of it all, and now, as they stood in this dark, forgotten room, everything that had happened between them felt like it was unraveling at the seams.

Damian's eyes flicked to hers, and for a moment, there was nothing between them but the weight of silence. His expression softened, just barely, before his lips parted.

"They're coming," he said, his voice low, gritty with the tension of the situation. "The people who've been hunting us. They won't stop until they get what they want."

Lena swallowed hard, the words landing like a weight in her chest. They had barely escaped the warehouse, ducking into this abandoned building on the edge of the city to hide. But there was no safety here—not from what was coming, not from the men who seemed to be closing in on them at every turn.

"I can't keep doing this," Lena said, her voice barely above a whisper, trembling with something she couldn't control. "I can't keep running. I can't keep trusting you, Damian. I don't even know who you really are."

The words stung more than she expected. The look on his face—one of pained understanding—cut deeper than she could have imagined. His gaze dropped to the floor, his shoulders stiffening as if her words had struck him harder than he was willing to admit.

"I'm not asking you to trust me, Lena," he said, his voice strained, almost raw. "But you need to understand something. This isn't just about us. It's about your father, and the things he left behind. Things that are bigger than you, than me. Than anything we can control."

She closed her eyes, the weight of his words crashing down on her. Her father. The name still felt like a dagger in her side. Every step she had taken toward the truth, every question she had asked, had only led her deeper into a world of secrets she wasn't prepared for. She had always thought she knew who her father was. But now, everything about him—the things he'd hidden, the connections he'd made—was spiraling out of control.

"I never wanted this," she whispered, her voice thick with the pain of the admission. "I never wanted any of this."

Damian's eyes softened, the hardness in them fading into something more vulnerable, something that caught her off guard. He stepped toward her, slowly, deliberately, as though every movement was calculated. And for a brief moment, she saw him for who he truly was—his armor of coldness slipping just enough for her to see the man beneath.

"I know," he said quietly, his voice rough with something deeper, something that made her chest tighten. "I never wanted to drag you into this, either. But you're already here, and now, there's no going back."

Lena's breath caught as he reached out, his hand brushing gently against her cheek. The touch was unexpected, tender in its simplicity, and it sent a shiver down her spine. His fingers lingered there, the heat of his skin searing her, grounding her in a moment of vulnerability that she wasn't ready for.

"Damian..." she whispered, her voice trembling, caught between the need for answers and the desire to distance herself from him.

His gaze darkened, and his fingers moved to trace the line of her jaw, a soft, intimate touch that sent sparks through her chest. She wanted to pull away, to shut herself off from the emotions swirling inside her, but his presence was too overpowering. His nearness, his touch, everything about him felt magnetic, impossible to ignore.

"You don't have to do this alone," Damian murmured, his voice barely a breath. "But you have to decide, Lena. What are you willing to risk? What are you willing to fight for?"

Lena's pulse quickened, and her throat went dry as she searched his face. She could feel the heat between them, the undeniable pull of something deeper than either of them had been willing to admit. The storm that had started between them all those weeks ago hadn't just been about survival—it had been about something else, something more complicated, something she was afraid to confront.

She had spent so much of her life building walls, keeping people at arm's length, refusing to trust anyone. But with Damian, it was different. He was dangerous, yes. But there was something in his eyes that made her believe he wasn't just a player in this game—he was the only one who had ever truly seen her. And that scared her more than the people chasing them.

Her breath caught in her chest as his thumb gently brushed against her lips, his gaze intense, hungry with something she couldn't name. For a moment, the world seemed to fall away. She could feel his heart beating in time with hers, the space between them shrinking, closing in on something neither of them was prepared for.

"Lena," he breathed, his voice hoarse with desire. "You have to decide. You have to decide what you want—what we can be."

Her heart hammered in her chest, and for a fleeting moment, the world around them seemed to shift. Her mind raced, the storm of emotions swirling inside her—fear, confusion, yearning. This wasn't supposed to happen. She wasn't supposed to feel this way. But as he leaned in, his lips barely brushing against hers, everything she thought she knew about herself began to unravel.

The kiss was soft at first, tentative, as if neither of them could believe this moment was actually happening. But then the tension between them snapped, and the kiss deepened, both of them giving in to the unspoken need that had been building for weeks, for months.

Lena's mind screamed at her to pull away, to stop this before it was too late. But the warmth of his mouth, the heat of his body, was too much. She was already too far gone.

And in that moment, she realized she wasn't just fighting for answers anymore. She was fighting for something deeper, something that would change everything.

Ten

The Battle Within

The city felt quieter than usual, the oppressive fog still clinging to the streets, wrapping the buildings in an eerie blanket. It was as though the world had decided to hold its breath, waiting for something to break the silence. Lena's heart raced in her chest, and every step she took toward the warehouse was heavy with the weight of her decision. She had never felt so conflicted, so torn between the desire to escape and the pull of something she couldn't name—a dark, dangerous pull that kept drawing her back to Damian.

Her fingers twitched at her side as she walked, the cold air biting at her skin, but it wasn't the chill of the night that made her feel this way. It was the storm that raged inside her. The confusion. The fear. And the undeniable desire that had burned between her and Damian, pulling them closer, even when every instinct told her to run.

Lena had barely slept the night before. The kiss, the heated touch, still lingered on her lips, its taste still fresh in her mouth. But it wasn't just the kiss. It was everything that had happened between them—the way he had looked at her, as if she were the only thing that mattered in the world. And yet, she knew better than to trust it. He was dangerous. She was tangled in his world now, whether she liked it or not.

She reached the edge of the warehouse, her boots scraping against the wet pavement as she slowed her pace. The large metal doors loomed in front of her, like the mouth of some monstrous creature waiting to swallow her whole. The faint smell of rust and oil filled her nostrils, mixing with the musty scent of old wood and dust that clung to the building. The door creaked as she pushed it open, stepping into the dim light that barely filtered through the cracks in the walls.

Damian was already inside, standing at the far end of the room, his back to her. The shadows wrapped around him like a second skin, making him seem both distant and present at the same time. She took a tentative step forward, her heart thudding in her chest as she closed the distance between them.

His posture stiffened slightly as he heard her approach, but he didn't turn around immediately. It was as if he was giving her space to make the decision, to decide what she was going to do next. The stillness in the room was almost suffocating, as if everything depended on this one moment.

"Lena," he said finally, his voice low, but there was something in it that made her stomach twist. Was it concern? Regret? She couldn't tell.

"I'm here," she replied, her voice barely above a whisper. She wasn't sure what she had expected—perhaps for him to turn and face her, for everything to feel clear. But instead, everything felt more uncertain than ever. There was something else in the air now. The tension between them was thick enough to choke on, and she could feel the weight of it pressing down on her shoulders, making it hard to breathe.

Damian slowly turned around, his eyes meeting hers, dark and unreadable. The air between them seemed to pulse with an energy that neither of them could escape. She couldn't help but notice how his gaze softened, how the hard edges of his expression cracked just enough to let her see the vulnerability beneath. It was fleeting, like a shadow that passed through him, but it was there.

"Lena, you don't have to do this," Damian said, his voice thick with something close to regret. "You don't have to be a part of this war. I never wanted this for you."

Lena took a step closer, her breath quickening with each movement. Her body was caught between two opposing forces—one pulling her away from him, telling her to run, to get as far away from him as possible, and the other, a deeper, undeniable pull that made her want to stay. Want to understand him. Want to trust him.

"What are you asking me to do, Damian?" Her voice was a mixture of anger and fear, the confusion in her chest rising like a storm. "I don't know what's happening. I don't know who to trust anymore."

He stepped closer, his gaze never leaving hers, his presence looming over her like a shadow she couldn't escape. "You don't have to trust anyone but yourself," he said quietly, the words so simple, yet carrying the weight of everything between them. "But you need to make a choice. You need to decide what you're willing to fight for."

Lena swallowed hard, her throat dry. She wanted to scream, to demand answers, to understand why she was even here. But instead, she found herself stepping closer to him, caught between the need for distance and the magnetic force that seemed to pull her toward him.

"I don't know how to choose," she said, her voice barely above a whisper. She had never felt more lost in her life, her heart torn between two things she couldn't control. "I don't even know what I'm fighting for."

Damian's face softened, the hardness that had guarded him for so long slipping away. He reached out, his hand brushing her arm lightly, the touch electric in its simplicity. It was a small thing, but it made Lena's heart skip a beat, the tension between them intensifying in a way she couldn't ignore.

"You're fighting for the truth," he said, his voice quiet, but firm. "You're fighting for what's left of your father's legacy. And you're fighting for yourself. Because no matter what happens, you need to be strong enough to walk through this, Lena. Strong enough to face what's coming."

Lena closed her eyes, her breath catching in her throat as his words washed over her. She wanted to be strong. She wanted to believe that she could handle whatever this was, but the fear still gnawed at her, the uncertainty clawing at her insides. She had never been faced with something so overwhelming, so impossible to understand.

When she opened her eyes, Damian was standing even closer, his presence overwhelming in the dim light of the warehouse. She could feel the heat of his body so close to hers, the weight of his touch lingering on her arm. The silence between them stretched out, thick and taut, as if the world had stopped turning for just a moment.

And then, as if the storm that had been brewing for so long had finally reached its peak, Damian's lips brushed against hers. The kiss was hesitant at first, a gentle press of his mouth against hers, as if waiting for her to pull away. But she didn't. She didn't pull away. Instead, she leaned into it, her hand resting on his chest as the kiss deepened, the connection between them burning brighter than before.

It wasn't just the heat of the kiss that made Lena's heart race. It was the weight of the decision that hung between them, the knowledge that this moment—this fragile, fleeting moment—could change everything. Could change her.

Damian pulled back slightly, his forehead resting against hers, his breath ragged. "Lena, I need you to decide. I need you to decide if you're willing to fight for this—fight for us."

Her chest tightened at the words, the weight of them pulling her under. She wanted to say yes. She wanted to choose him, to choose this dangerous path that seemed to offer both destruction and salvation. But part of her was terrified. Terrified of what the future held, terrified of what would happen if she let herself fall into this.

"I don't know," she whispered, her voice barely audible, the words catching in her throat. "I don't know if I'm strong enough."

"You are," Damian said, his voice low and insistent. "You're stronger than you think. And you don't have to do this alone."

Lena closed her eyes, feeling the weight of his words settle into her chest. She wanted to believe him. She wanted to believe that whatever this was—whatever connection they shared—could survive the storm that was coming.

But the question still hung in the air, unanswered: Was she ready to fight for it?

Eleven

A Love Rekindled

The moon hung low in the sky, a sliver of pale light barely breaking through the thick canopy of clouds. The streets of the city were quieter than usual, the familiar hum of life muffled beneath the weight of the evening's tension. It felt like the calm before the storm—everything suspended in a moment of fragile stillness. But Lena knew better than to trust the silence. The storm was coming, and this time, there would be no escaping it.

She stood on the apartment balcony, her arms crossed over her chest, gazing out at the city below. The wind whipped through her hair, tugging at the strands and making them dance around her face. Her breath formed clouds in the cold air, each exhale mingling with the fog that had descended on the city, shrouding everything in a misty veil. The world below her was a blur of motion, yet she felt like an outsider, watching it all unfold from a distance.

Lena had tried to push the memory of that night—the kiss, the words Damian had spoken—away. But they kept resurfacing, haunting her in the quiet moments when she was alone with her thoughts. The way his lips had tasted, the heat of his touch, the desperation in his eyes when he'd told her how important it was to make a choice. But what choice? What was she supposed to do now, knowing that everything about her life was a lie, knowing that the past was about to catch up with her in a way she couldn't predict?

She closed her eyes, her breath catching in her throat as she felt the weight of the uncertainty settle in her chest. The war that Damian had spoken of, the one her father had been a part of, was not just a distant memory. It was a living, breathing thing, and it was coming for her.

She wasn't sure how much longer she could stay on the sidelines, caught between two worlds—one that promised safety, and another that dragged her into darkness, pulling her further from the life she'd known. There was no escaping it now. No matter how much she wanted to turn away, to retreat into the safety of her old life, it was too late. She was already in this, tangled in a web of secrets, lies, and danger.

The sound of footsteps broke through her thoughts, and she didn't need to turn around to know who it was. Her pulse quickened at the mere thought of him—Damian. His presence had a way of slipping into her thoughts when she least expected it, like a shadow that clung to her skin.

She didn't move as he stepped onto the balcony behind her, his footsteps light on the wooden floor. The silence between them was thick, heavy with the weight of unspoken words, but it wasn't uncomfortable. It was familiar. His presence was a comfort and a curse, a constant reminder of the path she had chosen, whether she liked it or not.

"You're still here," Damian said quietly, his voice low and smooth, like velvet against her skin. He stepped closer, the warmth of his body radiating through the cold night air, but he didn't touch her. His presence was enough. It always had been.

Lena didn't answer immediately, instead choosing to focus on the city below, as if the answer to her turmoil could be found in the lights flickering in the distance. She had always believed she had control over her life, that the choices she made were hers to dictate. But that had never been true, not really. Every decision, every twist of fate had led her here, and now she was standing at the edge of something she couldn't see, couldn't fully understand.

"I didn't think I'd see you again," she said finally, her voice soft but carrying the weight of everything she was too afraid to admit. "After everything that's happened… I thought I'd be alone in this."

"You're not alone," Damian replied, his voice steady, but there was an underlying tension in it that told her more than he was willing to admit. She could feel the words hanging in the air between them, unspoken, yet understood. The storm that had been building between them was far from over. If anything, it was about to break wide open.

Lena turned slightly, just enough to glance at him from the corner of her eye. The dim light from the street below caught the sharp angles of his face, casting half of it in shadow, the other half in a soft glow. He was a figure of contradictions—cold and distant one moment, warm and protective the next. Every time she thought she had figured him out, he would do something that shifted her understanding of him, like a puzzle that constantly rearranged itself, defying her attempts to solve it.

"I don't know if I can keep doing this," she confessed, her voice barely a whisper. "I don't know if I'm strong enough to face whatever's coming."

Damian's eyes softened, and for the first time in a long while, she saw something vulnerable in him. The tough, impenetrable exterior that he had worn for so long seemed to crack just enough for her to glimpse the man beneath. He reached out, his fingers brushing against her arm, a light touch that sent a jolt of warmth through her.

"You're stronger than you think," he said softly, his gaze locking onto hers with an intensity that made her breath hitch. "I've seen it in you. You have a strength that I've never seen in anyone else."

Her chest tightened at his words, the sincerity in his voice making her heart race. She had never believed in herself the way he seemed to believe in her, and yet, in that moment, the weight of his belief was almost too much to bear. She wasn't sure she was strong enough for what was coming, for the storm that loomed just on the horizon. But his words, his touch, made her want to believe.

Lena turned fully to face him now, her eyes searching his for something more—something beyond the guarded, distant man she had come to know. What she found there, in the depths of his gaze, was a mixture of pain and something else—a longing, maybe. Something unspoken, buried beneath the surface, but undeniable.

"I don't know if I can trust you," she said, her voice trembling, the words heavy with doubt and fear. "You've kept so much from me. You've lied to me, Damian. And I don't know if I can keep living like this. I don't know if I can keep trusting you."

He took a step closer, his gaze unwavering, and for a moment, the world seemed to fall away. The space between them shrank until they were standing so close she could feel the heat of his body, hear the steady rhythm of his breath. He was close enough now that she could taste the faintest hint of whiskey on his lips, feel the pulse of his heartbeat as though it were her own.

"I never meant to hurt you," he whispered, his voice raw, more vulnerable than she had ever heard it. "I've been trying to protect you, even when I didn't know how. But I'm not asking for your trust, Lena. I'm asking for a chance."

A chance.

The words hung in the air between them, heavy with possibility. And as they stood there, in the quiet of the night, Lena felt the pull between them shift, deepen. There was no turning back from this. No more hiding behind the walls she had built to protect herself. She had already made her choice. She had already stepped into the storm with him, and there was no walking away now.

"I don't know what's ahead," she whispered, her voice thick with emotion. "But I know I can't face it without you."

Damian's expression softened, his hand coming up to cradle her face gently, his thumb brushing over her cheek as if memorizing the feel of her skin. The kiss that followed was slow, hesitant at first, as though both of them were testing the waters, unsure of how to move forward. But then it deepened, and everything else faded away—everything except the feeling of him against her, the warmth of his touch, the overwhelming pull that had always been there, even when they fought it.

For the first time in what felt like forever, Lena allowed herself to believe in something—believe that whatever came next, they would face it together.

Twelve

A New Dawn

The first rays of dawn filtered through the cracks in the blinds, casting a soft, golden glow over the room. The light was quiet, almost hesitant, as though it was too unsure what it would find. The city beyond the window was still, veiled in mist, with only the faint hum of distant traffic breaking the silence. Everything felt suspended in a fragile moment of peace, as if the storm that had threatened to tear everything apart was momentarily forgotten.

Lena sat on the edge of the bed, her hands clasped tightly in her lap, her mind racing with everything that had happened in the past few days. The choices she had made. The secrets she had uncovered. The promises Damian had made to her and the way his touch had ignited something within her that she wasn't sure she was ready to face. Every part of her wanted to escape, to run from it all and return to the safety of her old life. But she knew that wasn't possible anymore.

Her gaze drifted to the empty space beside her, where Damian had been only a few hours ago. He had left quietly, as always, disappearing into the shadows before she could fully process what had happened between them. The kiss. The promises. The unspoken bond that had formed between them threaded them together in a way neither could deny. She had tried to push it aside, to focus on the mission, but it was impossible. Damian had become something more than just an ally, more than just a guide through the labyrinth of danger and secrets. He had become part of her story, and no matter how much she tried to distance herself, she knew she couldn't undo it.

The door creaked open behind her, and Lena stiffened, her body instinctively tensing. She didn't need to look to know who it was. She could feel him—the pull of his presence, the familiar tension that seemed to follow him everywhere. The air shifted as Damian stepped into the room, his footsteps light but deliberate, the sound of them steady against the quiet hum of the morning.

"Lena," he said quietly, his voice low and hesitant, as though testing the waters between them. "I didn't want to wake you."

She turned her head, meeting his gaze, and the world seemed to stop for a moment. His dark eyes were tired, shadowed by something she couldn't quite name. There was a hardness to him, an edge that hadn't been there before. It was as if the weight of the world had finally caught up with him, and the facade of control he had worn so carefully for so long was beginning to crack.

"You didn't," Lena replied softly, her voice thick with the lingering emotions from the night before. "I wasn't sleeping."

Damian moved closer, his eyes never leaving hers. There was something in his gaze now, something raw and vulnerable that made her heart ache. She couldn't ignore it, couldn't pretend it wasn't there. Their connection had always been there, but now it was undeniable. It was woven into the very fabric of everything that had happened, everything they had shared. And no matter how hard she tried to resist it, it was too strong to break.

"I never wanted to pull you into this," he said, his voice tight, like the words were heavy on his tongue. "I've been trying to protect you from the beginning, but I don't know how to anymore."

Lena swallowed, her throat dry. "You've protected me in ways I didn't even understand," she admitted, her voice barely above a whisper. "But this… this is bigger than both of us. I don't know if I'm strong enough to face it, Damian."

He stepped closer, his hand reaching out as if to touch her, but then hesitating, his fingers curling into a fist at his side. The space between them felt like an invisible wall, and yet it was as if every inch of her skin was aware of the tension and the distance they had built between them in the wake of everything that had happened.

"You are," Damian said softly, his voice almost a prayer. "You don't have to do this alone."

Lena felt the weight of his words settle into her chest, a slow, steady pressure that left her breathless. She wanted to believe him and trust that this—whatever this was between them—wasn't just another trap. But every part of her wanted to run, to escape the chaos that had become her life. The truth was, she didn't know what she wanted anymore. She didn't know if she could keep fighting.

"You've made me believe in things I didn't think I could," she said, her voice thick with emotion. "But I don't know what's real anymore. I don't know if I can keep following this path."

Damian's hand moved then, reaching out and gently cupping her face, his thumb brushing over her cheek. His touch was soft, tender, as if trying to soothe the storm that raged inside her. His gaze never wavered from hers, and at that moment, everything else faded away. It was just the two of them, standing on the precipice of something they both knew was bigger than them.

"You're not alone in this," Damian repeated, his voice a low whisper, his breath warm against her skin. "I'll be with you every step of the way."

Lena's pulse quickened at the sincerity in his voice, and his touch made her feel safe and exposed simultaneously. There was no denying the connection between them or the way her body responded to his nearness. And yet, every instinct told her to pull away, to protect herself from the danger he brought with him.

She closed her eyes, fighting the wave of emotions that threatened to overwhelm her. Her chest felt tight, and her breath came in shallow gasps as she struggled to make sense of it all. This was a war, a battle that was already underway, and she had already been dragged into it. But the question remained: What was she willing to risk for the truth?

"You said you wanted to protect me," Lena said, her voice breaking through the fog of uncertainty in her mind. "But you're part of this. You're part of the war that's coming. And I'm not sure I can trust that anymore."

Damian's hand dropped from her face, his jaw tightening as he stepped back. For a moment, he seemed to be weighing her words, his eyes searching hers, as if trying to read the depths of her soul.

"I'm not asking you to trust me," he said, his voice hoarse. "I'm asking you to trust us. To trust what we can be, what we're building together. There's no way out of this, Lena. Not for either of us. But I'm not asking you to face it alone."

Lena felt her chest tighten at his words. There was a promise in them, a promise that both terrified and comforted her. She didn't know if she was ready for what was coming, didn't know if she could bear the weight of the choices ahead. But one thing was clear: whatever happened, whatever choices they made, she wasn't going to face it alone.

"I'm not asking for a way out," she said, her voice quiet but steady. "I'm asking for the truth."

Damian's eyes softened, the hard edge to his expression finally giving way to something else—something softer. He reached out again, his hand brushing gently against hers, the contact sending a jolt of warmth through her.

"You'll have it," he whispered. "The truth, Lena. All of it. We'll face it together."

For the first time in what felt like forever, Lena allowed herself to believe in the possibility of something more than survival. For the first time, she allowed herself to believe that maybe, just maybe, she wasn't alone in this fight.

And as the dawn broke fully across the sky, the first light of day spilling across the room, Lena knew that whatever came next—whatever battle awaited them—she would face it with Damian at her side.

www.ingramcontent.com/pod-product-compliance
Lightning Source LLC
LaVergne TN
LVHW020431080526
838202LV00055B/5128